# The Best of
# PUNCH
## Cartoons in Colour

Thanks (once again) to Andre Gailani of Punch Cartoon Library
for all his help with this book

Published in 2012 by Prion
An imprint of the Carlton Publishing Group
20 Mortimer Street
London W1T 3JW

1 3 5 7 9 10 8 6 4 2

Editorial Manager: Roland Hall
Design Manager: Stephen Cary
Design: Chris Francis
Production: Dawn Cameron

A CIP catalogue record for this book is available from the British Library

ISBN 978-1-85375-856-0

Printed in Dubai

*Previous page:* Quentin Blake, 1988
*Opposite:* George Sprod, 1953
*Page 8:* F H Townsend, 1920

# The Best of
# PUNCH
## Cartoons in Colour

Edited by

## Helen Walasek

Foreword by

## Quentin Blake

PRION

# CONTENTS

# FOREWORD
## by Quentin Blake

It's a pleasure to be asked to write something about coloured pictures in *Punch* and to cover *Punch* covers too. The only problem, I suppose, is how to do it without sounding too much like some sort of superannuated old-timer. "Why, I remember the time ..." Nothing else for it I suppose, because I do remember the time.

I remember the time when I first encountered *Punch*. (You never called it *Punch* magazine; it was always just *Punch*). It was when I was a schoolboy in mid-20th century London suburbia, and I was sent (probably in short trousers) to the local barber's shop to have my hair cut. It was cut too short and then varnished on top like a sort of shiny crust. The consolation was that as there was always some time to wait when I could look at the well-thumbed copies of *Punch* lying about for the clients' perusal. The unusual feature of *Punch* at that time was that it had exactly the same black-and-white cover every week – only the date was changed – and not only that but, as I later discovered, the paper had been using the same cover every week for the past hundred years. It was drawn by Dicky Doyle, a precocious and gifted artist much admired ever since by cartoonists and illustrators; and if it couldn't last for ever it had a good run for its money and in some ways set the tone and approach for what eventually followed.

In those days it was only the Christmas and perhaps some other very special number that came out with a specially commissioned coloured cover; but in the developing post-war scene more and more pretexts for special covers were discovered and in the end the "ordinary" cover came to look just too pale and undernourished. Part of me was sad to see it go, but the rest of me was absolutely delighted. Bliss was it in that dawn to be alive, but be young-and-if-you-had-only-had-small-black-and-white-drawings-

in-the-paper-so-far was very heaven. Perhaps I exaggerate. It was nevertheless a wonderful opportunity. Some of the covers were commissioned for special occasions, but many were just submitted. In some sense a formula was already established, because the traditional *Punch* figure, attended by Toby the dog, needed to be well to the fore, and you set about finding a new twist or situation. What a pleasure to discover how one could make, for instance, that hooked nose and chin look like a lobster's claw … And as far as I was concerned it was also, as each cover stood on its own, the chance to experiment – with pastels, quills, collage – and of course get paid for it.

The other great pleasure was to see those stars of the paper that one had admired in black-and-white go into colour. George Sprod, for instance. (To begin with I used to think that his signature, Sprod, was one of those names that cartoonists sometimes make up for themselves, until I met him: a clever, pawky Australian who seemed to have a special insight into the British way of life). Or the elegant, wonderfully decorative Michael ffolkes. (By contrast he had invented the name that perfectly suited his art. When I first met him I was baffled to know how he came to be married to Mrs Brian Davis). Or Rowland Emett, with the intensely English romantic eccentricity of his world of outdated railways. Or Ronald Searle, already established as *Punch*'s most brilliant theatre caricaturist, but masterly in any situation. And also, something of a revelation to me as a young artist, the bizarre, rich, painterly covers of the French artist, André François ....

But sorry, this old-timer is becoming garrulous in his reminiscences, and what you want to do is to be allowed to look at the pictures in colour and in peace. Please, find your own favourites. It's a treat.

*Quentin Blake, London 2012*

George Sprod, 1956

No. 6186          PUNCH, MARCH 4 1959          Vol. CCXXXVI

Quentin Blake, 1959

# INTRODUCTION

## by Helen Walasek

Starting life on July 17, 1841 in the heady years of early Victorian publishing, *Punch* began as a radically-inclined satirical magazine which delighted in puncturing Establishment attitudes; by the start of the 20th century it had settled into an altogether more comfortable existence as National Institution. Always funny – never vulgar – the memorable images of its cartoons had become deeply embedded not only in the British cultural consciousness, but had made their impact across the wider world. Conservative though it may have become editorially, part of the reason behind *Punch*'s success (and longevity) was its ability to package itself in new formats and experiment with the latest production methods. By the early 1900s colour began moving onto the magazine's pages – first on the covers of its yearly Christmas Almanacks, with the occasional two-colour spread of Bernard Partridge's political caricatures inside. Standing out from a sea of black and white print, these colour covers were adored by bookstall managers – *Punch*'s advertisers, too, were keen to have their ads printed in colour. It was a concept that was set to expand.

The magazine had tinkered with the idea of a Summer Number to join the Almanack shortly before the outbreak of the First World War. Put on hold until after the conflict, however, it was not until 1920 that *Punch*'s first Summer Number was produced. Most exciting of all for readers (and for the magazine's artists), it was the first issue to include full colour illustrations. With their full-page drawings the Almanacks had become a chance for the magazine's artists to pull out all the stops; now, freed from the limitations of black and white, the opportunity to create works in colour inspired them to even greater heights. And there were spectacular results: Fougasse's pared down drawings explode into unexpectedly brilliant Jazz Age hues, while Arthur Watts – king of the bird's-eye view – shows his mastery of watercolour, as well as of pen and ink. And H M Bateman's goggle-eyed characters seem even more ferocious in colour. E H Shepard, illustrator *extraordinaire*, produced some of his best colour work ever: wonderful double page spreads, a bouquet of charming illustrations to poems by Evoe (E V Knox), and the quirky accompaniments to Jan Struther's *The Modern Struwwelpeter*. Yet today *Punch*'s early colour art is all but forgotten.

Far from depressing output, the outbreak of the Second World War seemed to spur *Punch*'s artists on – Shepard

painted two of his most brilliant double page spreads: *Spring Reconaissance* of 1940 and *Noise 1841 / Noise 1941*. But the most dramatic image of *Punch*'s war was certainly Leslie Illingworth's *The Combat* of 1940; his illustration of a solitary RAF fighter pilot confronting the monstrous sky-darkening Nazi foe brought postbags full of heartfelt letters from readers. Wartime paper rationing affected production and as the war went on the magazine's paper became coarser, the print quality blotchier, the number of pages cut. But legend had it that *Punch* was considered so essential to the war effort it was granted an extra paper allowance and better quality paper was found for the special numbers and their colour inserts.

Nevertheless, a 1942 advertisement warned readers to place orders for the Summer Number with their newsagent immediately – only a limited number were to be printed due to the paper restrictions. Forced to cut back on its planned centenary publications in 1941 because of the war, *Punch* used the Festival of Britain in 1951 as a properly celebratory occasion to produce a special issue packed with colour illustrations, reprising it in 1953 with a delightful souvenir number for the young Queen Elizabeth's coronation.

One feature of the weekly issues, however, had remained sacrosanct for over 100 years, despite regular updating of the magazine's design, layout and content: the classic 1849 Richard 'Dicky' Doyle cover. When maverick new broom Malcolm Muggeridge was appointed editor of *Punch* in 1953 and began making changes, many thought the traditional (and now rather fusty looking) cover would be first to go. But there was no overnight revolution. Muggeridge introduced alterations gradually, allowing artists the occasional riff on the iconic design (in black, white and red), the odd colour painting. Then on October 10, 1956 a full colour illustration by Norman Thelwell of a 'Thelwell pony' and its miniature rider clearing a fence, with Mr Punch and Toby looking on, appeared on the cover and the Doyle drawing disappeared forever. Covers thereafter changed weekly and a new opportunity opened for artists to showcase their work – now to be commissioned for a *Punch* cover became the Holy Grail of cartoonists and illustrators.

At first the brief for the covers had a single requirement on subject matter: that Mr Punch appear somewhere in the picture (with dog Toby also welcome). The magazine's artists were soon adept at interpreting this in a variety of ingenious ways. Over the next decade there followed an astonishing array of covers by some of the world's finest illustrators. Many were regular contributors like Ronald Searle, Quentin Blake, Russell Brockbank, Norman Thelwell, André François, Sempé, George Adamson, PAV, Kenneth Mahood and Ralph Steadman. But others who were not, such as the Polish-born graphic artist Jan Le Witt of the Lewitt-Him design partnership and David McKee (later famous for his children's books), produced some of the magazine's most idiosyncratic covers.

However, times were changing and *Punch*'s circulation was in a slow decline after the highpoint of the 1950s. There were still wonderful covers in the 1970s by artists like the superb caricaturist Trog (Wally Fawkes), John Jensen, Geoffrey Dickinson and Ed McLachlan, but colour reproduction disappeared inside the magazine for years altogether. When four-colour printing became the norm in the 1980s, colour returned to *Punch*'s editorial pages. The second half of the 1980s and the early 1990s proved to be a golden age of cartooning in the magazine with artists like Mike Williams, Stan Eales, Robert Wilson and old hand Ed McLachlan among the best of the colourists. Still the Gold Standard for cartoonists and illustrators, *Punch* was nevertheless finding it hard to carry in the now highly competitive magazine trade, even with its widely-reported 150th anniversary celebrations

on July 17, 1991, which included a rambunctious parody of the Dicky Doyle cover by Ralph Steadman for a special collector's issue. Just a few months later, on April 8, 1992 the last issue of 'old' *Punch* was published. It began with a cover by Holte – one of the most magnificent ever – depicting Mr Punch, wife Judy and dog Toby waving farewell as they trudged towards the setting sun. Though the magazine was re-launched in 1996 with many *Punch* stalwarts contributing, it could not survive in the new environment and closed for good in 2002.

The legend of *Punch* cartoons lives on – but its spectacular illustrations in colour have been all but forgotten. So for here for the very first time we've brought together the best of that remarkable collection, a feast of pictorial treats in full glorious colour. We've gathered hundreds of classic works from the 1920s to the 1990s – most never reproduced since their original publication. There are illustrations, covers and cartoons by some of the world's greatest artists. A few are old favourites, like Sillince's harried businessman and his serene gardener and Williams' hibernating bear tempted by the last of the Mohicans, but most are unknown and waiting to be discovered by the lucky readers of this book.

*Helen Walasek, London 2012*

9

SPRING...

... RECONAISSANCE

E H Shepard, 1940

10

Henry Mayo Bateman, 1924

THE PLUMBER'S PARADISE.

WHEN BOTTICELLI BINNS DEVOTED SO MUCH THOUGHT TO THE REPAINTING OF HIS HOUSE, I DON'T THINK HE COULD
HAVE HEARD OF THE PROPOSAL TO—

ERECT A NEW PILLAR-BOX IN FRONT OF IT.

12

THE OUTSIDER.

Arthur Watts, 1934

# A Fitte of the Blues

The Swain.
"To-night the ecstasy is dead
That winged our shimmering
shoes."
The Nymph.
"To-night creation is not red."
The Swain.
"To-night we dance the Blues."

The Nymph,
"All lovely things are doomed to
dust."
The Swain.
"The hey-day of the jazz
Was practically bound to bust."
The Nymph.
"And bust the hey-day has."

The Swain.
"When I recall the close embrace
Wherein we two were knit—"

The Nymph.
"When I recall the fatuous face
That always went with it "

The Swain.
"When I recall the feverish
joys
Of many a room wherein
We circled slowly "
The Nymph. "To the noise
Of negroes hammering tin—"

The Swain.
"I cannot speak without regret
For what the world must lose."
The Nymph.
"In time perhaps—"
The Swain. "I may forget."
The Nymph
"Then come, we'll dance the
Blues." EVOE.

13

Ernest Howard Shepard, 1924

# Fougasse (Kenneth Bird) (1887–1965)

A *Punch* contributor from 1916, Bird became its art editor in 1937 and editor in 1949. Best known for the minimalist squiggles of his drawings and the WWII propaganda campaign *Careless Talk Costs Lives*, his colour works for *Punch* could be exuberant and far from understated.

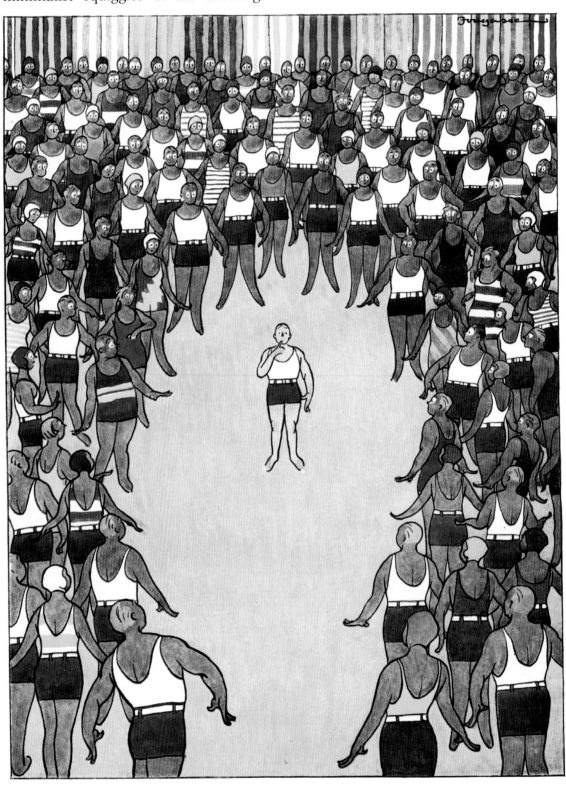

THE COLOUR QUESTION.

THE NEW ARRIVAL ON THE BATHING-BEACH.

NOW WHO SAYS THAT WE'RE NOT A MUSICAL NATION?

Fougasse (Kenneth Bird), 1929

MISS PRISCILLA BROWNE BEGAN HER DAY WITH A
LITTLE GENTLE EXERCISE,

SO DOES HER GREAT-GRAND-DAUGHTER.

16

AFTER WHICH SHE WOULD ENJOY A MODEST BATHE,

HER GREAT-GRAND-DAUGHTER ALSO BATHES.

# EIGHTY YEARS OF CHANGE.

OF AN AFTERNOON SHE WOULD TAKE A PROMENADE
WITH AN ELIGIBLE YOUNG MAN,

WHILE HER GREAT-GRAND-DAUGHTER GOES OFF WITH
ANYTHING THAT BLOWS ALONG.

17

SHE FINISHED THE DAY BY STEPPING A QUADRILLE
AT THE ASSEMBLY ROOMS,

AND HER GREAT-GRAND-DAUGHTER FOX-TROTS IN
THE HOTEL LOUNGE.

Lewis Baumer, 1921

18

THE SPOIL-SPORT

R, THE CULPRIT WHO ADMITTED EVERYTHING.

Henry Mayo Bateman, 1923

# A FACE IN THE SUN.

ARE YOU FEELING BLUE?

THEN TRY GRILLEM—THAT'S THE PLACE FOR SUNSHINE.

GO ON THE PIER—

AND BY—

THE TIME—

YOU REACH—

THE END—

YOU WON'T KNOW YOURSELF.

20

Frank Reynolds, 1925

THE KILLJOY.

Fougasse (Kenneth Bird), 1927

# SANTA CLAUS

"IN Lapland where the reindeer grow
There is a huge amount of snow."
*"Dear father! is that all you know?"*

\* \* \* \*

The up-to-date and modern child
Does not consent to be beguiled
With mere romance on Christmas-time
Made up in prose, still less in rhyme ;
But when the tinkling sleighbells sound
And Santa Claus comes on his round—
Remembering from his Nature-books
Far more than how the reindeer looks—
He bids his brother rise from bed
And knocks some sense into his head.

"Consider, Conrad," he observes,
" The palmate antlers with their curves,
The heavy structure and the bland eye
Of these *Rangiferi tarandi.*
How fitted are the hairy hoofs
For running swiftly over roofs !
How suitable the hairy nose
To prod with in the Lapland snows
For lichens which replace the loss
Of summer's food with reindeer-moss !
The antlers of the female kind
Are smaller than the males, we find ;
The creature is extremely strong ;
The hair in winter-time grows long.
It roams about in largish herds,
Producing milk and also curds.
The reindeer is to Lapland, note,
A horse, a cow, a sheep, a goat ;
It gives them clothing, food and health
And constitutes, in fact, their wealth.
To us the reindeer also brings
No end of interesting things ;
This train, for instance, which is yours,
To move by clockwork on our floors,
With quantities of extra line,
And this small camera, which is mine."

So saying, the ingenious boy
Removes from Santa Claus each toy,
And nothing less concerns him than
To talk to the old gentleman.

\* \* \* \*

" In Lapland, where the reindeer grow,
There is a huge amount of snow."
*"Dear father! is that all you know?'*

EVOE.

22

E. H. Shepard

Ernest Howard Shepard, 1925

Arthur Watts, 1931

BRIGHTER PRESENTS.

"AND THERE'S A NICE LITTLE BOOK ON PICASSO FOR *YOU*. LAURA."

REMARKABLE OCCURRENCE IN THE HEART OF THE METROPOLIS.
THE NEWCOMERS TO FLAT NO. 21 USE THEIR BALCONY AS A BALCONY.

Fougasse (Kenneth Bird), 1928

THE DRIVE.

Henry Mayo Bateman, 1932

25

# Punch in People

Continuing its tradition of celebrity caricatures, Punch printed a superb series of collectables over 1934–1935. The personalities came from the arts, science, politics and media, through to Montagu Norman (opposite), governor of the Bank of England and Stenson Cooke of the Automobile Association. The others depicted here are veteran actress Marie Tempest, the Viceroy of India Lord Willingdon, the Lord Chancellor, Viscount Hailsham, and John Reith of the BBC (*see* page 31).

*Essex (F Roberts Johnson), 1935*

*The Brain of the 'A A'.*

*George Whitelaw, 1935*

*Fifty Years a Favourite.*

*Robert Stewart Sherriffs, 1935*

*Mars in Panoply.*

*Ernest Howard Shepard, 1934*

*Lord Willingdon and Friend.*

ESSEX

*The Governor.*

Essex (F Roberts Johnson), 1935

THE PRIZEWINNING STATION.

Harold William Hailstone, 1935

29

Frank Reynolds, 1926

30

"WHAT WE WANT, JOE, IS FOR SOMEBODY TO COME AN' TURN THIS 'ERE PLACE INTO ONE CF THESE 'ERE PALM BEACHES."

Essex (F Roberts Johnson), 1934

*Prospero.*

"The isle is full of noises, sounds, and sweet airs, that give delight.

WE WERE BORED TO TEARS WITH THESE SUN-BAKED CROWDS AT DEAUVILLE AND ANTIBES—

34

SO WE WENT FURTHER AFIELD AND TRIED THE COAST OF AFRICA, ONLY TO FIND CONGESTED SEASIDE-RESORTS—

# IN SEARCH OF FRESH FIELDS AND SEABOARDS NEW.

SO WE STEAMED AWAY TO THE SOUTH SEA ISLANDS, BUT EVEN THERE WE FOUND FAR TOO MANY PEOPLE ABOUT.

AT LAST WE DISCOVERED A RECENT VOLCANIC ISLAND WHICH IS LIKELY TO SINK AGAIN IN A DAY OR TWO, SO
PROBABLY WON'T ATTRACT TOO LARGE A CROWD.

Arthur Wallis Mills, 1930

THE DANCING-GIRL'S PARADISE.

Henry Mayo Bateman, 1925

William Leigh Ridgewell, 1935

"I SAY, DO YOU HAPPEN TO HAVE ONE OF THE SORT THAT SQUEAKS?"

37

# SARTORIAL TENNIS.

LOVE—FIFTEEN . . . .

LOVE—THIRTY . . . .

LOVE—FORTY . . . .

GAME.

Fougasse (Kenneth Bird), 1923

George Morrow, 1930

LITTLE WILLIE JONES, WITH A BENT PIN, WINS THE FIRST PRIZE IN THE ANNUAL SEA-FISHING COMPETITION AT
PADDLEBEACH PIER.

Arthur Watts, 1929

*Fisherman (in extremely sophisticated Cornish town).* "AH, FOLLOWING IN THE FOOTSTEPS OF VAN GOGH, SIR!"

Frank Reynolds, 1936

TWO ASPECTS OF TRIUMPH.

Harold William Hailstone, 1935

"YES, MY DEAR, THINGS HAVE CHANGED A LOT . . . WHY, I REMEMBER WHEN THIS USED TO
BE THE OLD GIRLS' FRIENDLY SOCIETY."

George Morrow, 1934

THE SPARTAN SWIMMING CLUB VISITS THE ARCTIC CIRCLE IN SEARCH OF
SUITABLE WEATHER CONDITIONS.

# Arthur Watts (1883–1935)

Usually to be relied upon for drawing a scene from an unusual perspective, Arthur Watts was also an accomplished watercolourist. Watts contributed regularly to *Punch* from 1921 until his premature death in a plane crash over the Swiss Alps in 1935.

*The Guide.* "TAKE IT EASY, SIR, AND KEEP YOUR STRENGTH FOR THE DIFFICULT PART."

Arthur Watts, 1931

*The Bargee.* "AND WHERE DID *YOU* COME FROM BABY DEAR?"

## HERE AND THERE.

OH, bother this absurd taxation
　That makes us have to go and roam
Through all our summer-tide vacation
　Beside the deep Atlantic foam !

With what despair and utter loathing
　We strip upon the sunlit beach ;
We have no stylish water clothing
　And so "abroad"'s beyond our reach.

The sea, of course, is *much*, much damper
　In England, and one has to walk,
Or even run about and scamper,
　Instead of sitting down to talk.

But in those lovely foreign places
　In dressing up to take a dip
One gets away from wind-swept spaces
　Which give one, so to speak, the pip.

The fashionable tide caresses
　The smart and most exclusive shore ;
One wears the most delightful dresses
　And bathing *never* seems to bore.
　　　　　　　　　　　EVOE.

46

Ernest Howard Shepard, 1925

Charles Grave, 1933

TRAFFIC CONTROL ON THE HIGH SEAS.

DEVICE FOR ENABLING THE SUPER-GIANT LINER OF THE FUTURE TO GET ACROSS THE CHANNEL IN SAFETY.

48

49

Harold William Hailstone, 1936

"YES, THANKS, WE HAD A MARVELLOUS HOLIDAY, B-B-BUT I'M AFRAID WE L-LEFT IT A BIT L-LATE STARTING BACK."

CHRISTMAS

IN SOHO.

51

Frank Reynolds, 1930

Arthur Watts, 1934

"OH, DO STOP GRUMBLING, ARTHUR. YOU WANTED AN OLD-FASHIONED CHRISTMAS
AND NOW YOU'VE GOT ONE."

## CHRISTMAS PUDDING.

SIXPENCE for money,
  A ring to be wed,
But thimbles are old maids,
  Pamela said.

We stirred and we stirred it,
  Especially me,
And we all wished our hardest
  What we would be.

Pam's the best dancer,
  Joan's good at sums,
But *I* want the thimble
  We stirred with the plums.

Money and marriage
  May both be a sell,
But I do the hemstitch
  Most *frightfully* well.
                    EVOE.

53

Ernest Howard Shepard, 1927

THE NEW COCKTAIL.

Arthur Wallis Mills, 1934

A MASCOT ROMANCE.

James Henry Dowd, 1933

BATHING WAS ONCE A VERY SIMPLE AFFAIR. A YOUNG LADY WOULD HIRE HER COSTUME, RETIRE INTO HER MACHINE, TAKE A DISCREET DIP, AND THERE WAS AN END TO IT.

56

NOW-A-DAYS, IF ONE GOES ON THE SANDS—

ONE HAS TO BE PREPARED FOR ANYTHING—

OR HARDLY ANYTHING.

Lewis Baumer, 1931

58

AS ADVERTISED ;
OR, THE BULB CATALOGUE THAT FULFILLED ITS PROMISE.

William Leigh Ridgewell, 1932

## THE MANTLE OF WU

The dress that Joan has on to-day
    Was worn by Wu the Mandarin ;
Who put it on down Pekin way
    To read his old *Confucius* in.

There is no difference in the gown ;
    It still continues to provide
A rather lovely reach-me-down ;
    But what a change there is inside !

How strange to think the self-same robe
    That ugly Wu was wont to wear
Has travelled round the teeming globe
    To Joan the exquisitely fair !

How strange to think the outworn weeds
    Of one by whom so much was known
Of wise old books and ancient creeds
    Should decorate my darling Joan !

59

Ernest Howard Shepard, 1924

# The Royal Family I
## The Prince and the Princesses

From almost its very first issue *Punch* depicted the Royal Family on its pages, moving from irreverent to reverent and back. Here Bernard Partridge portrays the glamorous Prince of Wales tending the Imperial garden not long before he became king. Less than three years later Albert Edward had abdicated, and on the eve of their parent's coronation as King and Queen, the little Princesses Elizabeth and Margaret Rose were saluted by *Punch* in this charming fantasy by Thomas Derrick.

*Our Royal Gardener.*

Bernard Partridge, 1934

ANOTHER CORONATION

Thomas Derrick, 1937

THE FLOWERS AND THE PRINCESSES

62

THE CONTINUOUS PERFORMANCE.

Arthur Watts, 1932

THE BEAUTY-DOCTOR.

Arthur Watts, 1930

# TACTFUL ANSWERS TO GARDENING CORRESPONDENTS.

*COLONEL.*—WE ARE VERY GLAD TO HEAR OF YOUR SATISFACTION WITH THE LADY-GARDENER YOU ENGAGED THROUGH OUR COLUMNS. WE WERE CAREFUL TO SELECT A SPECIALIST, FEELING THAT A PLAINER TYPE OF GARDENER WOULD NOT SUIT YOU SO WELL.

*FED-UP.*—WE SUSPECT THAT YOU ARE CORRECT IN YOUR SURMISE CONCERNING THE PARTIAL CLEARANCE OF THE STRAWBERRY-BED IN YOUR ABSENCE. IT PROBABLY *WAS* THOSE BIRDS.

# TACTFUL ANSWERS TO GARDENING CORRESPONDENTS.

HEAD GARDENER.—NO DOUBT IT WAS A GREAT DISAPPOINTMENT TO YOU TO FIND THAT YOUR FAVOURITE SHOW BLOSSOM HAD BEEN PICKED, AND IN THE CIRCUMSTANCES IT IS QUITE INTELLIGIBLE THAT YOU SHOULD BE LOOKING OUT FOR ANOTHER SITUATION.

GARDEN LOVER.—WE ARE ALWAYS PLEASED TO ANSWER ANY QUERY FROM OUR READERS. FROM YOUR DESCRIPTION YOUR GARDEN IS TOO EXPOSED. LET YOUR HEDGE GROW ANOTHER FOUR FEET AND YOU WILL HAVE ALL THE PROTECTION YOU REQUIRE.

Arthur Wallis Mills, 1931

SEEING RED.

THE SIGN-PAINTER REGISTERS EMOTION.

Ernest Howard Shepard, 1933

Fougasse (Kenneth Bird), 1938

"COO, LOOK—THERE'S A CYCLIST!"

BE-whiskered and be-
bustled,
    Entwined about with
        plants.
Daguerreotypes unhustled
    Of uncles and of aunts!
With lamplight to illumine
    us
        How oft we had to look
At relatives albuminous
    Imbedded in a book!

Above their faded poses,
    Inquiring whose was
        whom's,
We bent obedient noses
    In slumberous drawing-
        rooms;

The horror of that
    memory,
    The faces proud and chill
(So Edward-ish and
    Emma-ry!) —
    It lingers with me still.

Now every aunt is brisker
    Than every niece, they
        say;
No uncle wears a whisker,
    And life is much more
        gay.
When evening brings the
    movie near
    The nephews howl with
        glee—
In fact their favourite
    souvenir
    Is photographs of me!
                    EVOE.

Ernest Howard Shepard, 1930

George Morrow, 1935

*The Specialist.* "THIS IS VERY INTERESTING, BUT I MUST NOT FORGET THAT I CAME HERE TO COLLECT SPECIMENS OF LEPIDOPTERA."

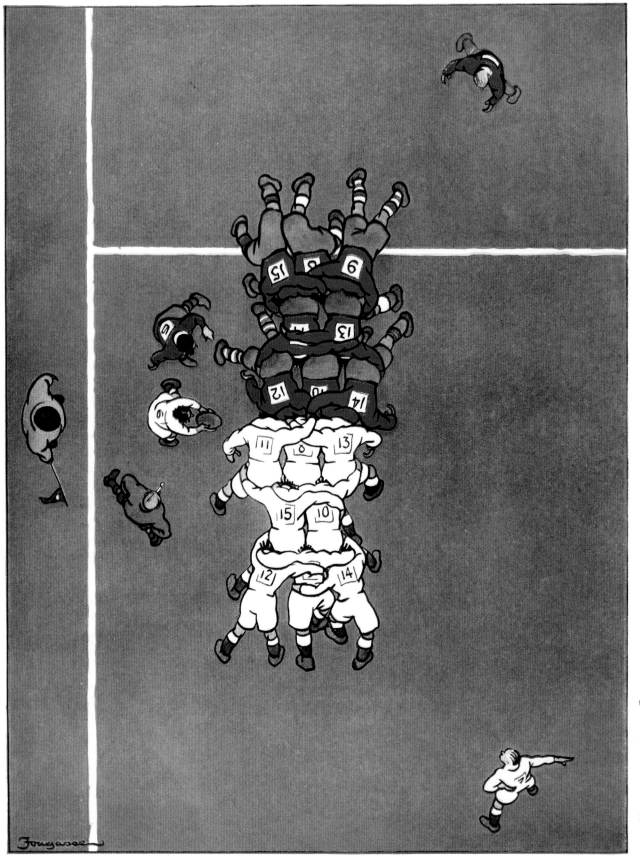

ALL THE SAME, YOU KNOW, THOSE AEROPLANES THAT FLY OVER TWICKENHAM MUST GET RATHER A JOLLY VIEW
OF THE GAME.

Fougasse (Kenneth Bird), 1932

Arthur Watts, 1933

"COO—ER, PERCE! DON'T YOU WISH YOU WAS AN AIRMAN?"

"JUST RUN 'OME AN' FETCH ME MY SMALL 'AMMER, ALBERT."

Arthur Watts, 1929

73

Leslie Illingworth, 1933

*Man with particular grievance.* "OH, IT'S ONLY YOU, IS IT? I THOUGHT IT WAS ONE OF THOSE CONFOUNDED MOTOR-CYCLES KICKING UP A ROW AGAIN."

# Frank Reynolds (1876–1953)

Among *Punch*'s most prolific artists, Reynolds replaced F H Townsend as art editor in 1920. A traditional old-fashioned illustrator and a master of technique, Reynolds could be rather conservative in style, yet he produced some of his most inventive work during the Second World War while in his sixties.

THE STILL-LIFE SPECIALIST PAINTS A PORTRAIT.

Frank Reynolds, 1936

No. 5 CHANGES HANDS AND GOES GAY.

William Leigh Ridgewell, 1935

Arthur Watts, 1935

"I'LL TAKE THE SHOVE - HA'PENNY SCORE ALONG WITH US, OLD MAN. YOU'RE JUST NINE HUNDRED
POUNDS DOWN ON THE TEN YEARS WE'VE BEEN HERE."

Ernest Howard Shepard, 1929

## THE RUNAWAY GIRL.

POOR great-grandmother 's gone away
  From her place by old Sir Peter,
Poor great-grandmother 's gone to stay
With a millionaire from the U.S.A.
  Who 's awfully pleased to meet her.

Old Sir Peter is simply mad
  Over the flight of his daughter;
"The girl is a regular jade, egad!
To leave the excellent home she had
  For a place where the men drink
    water!"

But if one night by the firelight flame,
  When the gale blew loud in the
    Channel,
Poor great-grandmother suddenly came,
I 'm sure Sir Peter would leave his
    frame
  And welcome her back to her panel.
                                    EVOE.

79

Ernest Howard Shepard, 1927

"I KNOW. THINGS BEGAN TO GO WRONG AT DINNER. I WISH NOW THAT I'D GIVEN THAT EXTRA SHILLING A BOTTLE FOR THE CHAMPAGNE."

THE CUCKOO—AND THE JAY.

William Leigh Ridgewell, 1934

George Morrow, 1942

*" Yes, we allowed one of our artist customers to work off his overdraft."*

83

Frank Reynolds, 1937

OVERDUE

84

David Louis Ghilchik, 1930

## THE ART OF GOING ONE BETTER.
LEADER OF FASHION APPEARS WITH THE PERFECT BATHING-ANIMAL.

PUNCH

SUMMER NUMBER
1936

George Morrow, 1936

Paul Crum (Roger Pettiward), 1940

**SOME NORTHERN ANIMALS IN THEIR SUMMER AND WINTER DRESS**

(*With apologies to the Natural History Museum*)

Leslie Illingworth, 1937

SUNDAY AT LLANCULGWN

THE BOOK OF BEAUTY.

AS IT WAS IN GREAT-GRANDMAMA'S TIME YOU WERE EITHER A BLONDE OR A BRUNETTE
AND YOU LEFT IT AT THAT.

88

NOWADAYS, THANKS TO THE ADVANCEMENT OF CHEMICAL SCIENCE.

IT COULD CONTAIN CONSIDERABLY MORE VARIETY

AND WHAT IS MORE, THE SAME YOUNG LADY COULD POSE FOR THE LOT.

Lewis Baumer, 1937

"DON'T YOU REALISE THAT I'VE *GOT* TO BE AT 76, THE GROVE, BY EIGHT O'CLOCK?"

Pont (Graham Laidler), 1937

Leslie Illingworth, 1937

". . . SO I SAID YES, MRS. WIMPLESTRAW, I SAID, I THOUGHT I *WAS* VERY PARTIAL TO SAGO-PUDDING, I SAID. BUT THE SAGO-PUDDING *I'M* USED TO, I SAID, DOESN'T TASTE LIKE WARMED-UP CODS' EYES AND TREACLE, MRS. WIMPLESTRAW, I SAID. AND *THAT* SEEMED TO GET HER BACK UP—SEE? . . ."

"Look what I've brought you, darling—Roses!"

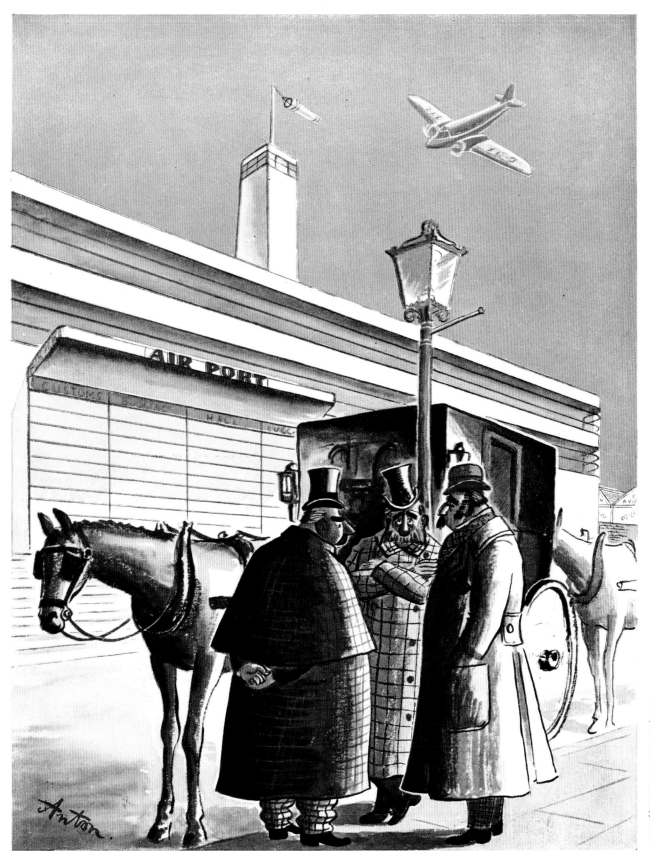

93

Anton (Antonia Yeoman), 1939

# Leslie Illingworth (1902–1979)

Illingworth became famous for his political cartoons for *Punch* and the *Daily Mail*. But his first contributions to *Punch* in the 1930s were of social subjects, among them his subtly toned watercolours for the magazine's special numbers.

94

THE NOVICE

Leslie Illingworth, 1940

Leslie Illingworth, 1934

*Bungalow Owner.* "YES, OLD MAN, I'LL GRANT YOU THEY DON'T LOOK VERY PRETTY, BUT HOW ELSE CAN ONE GET ANY PRIVACY ALONGSIDE THE MAIN ROAD NOWADAYS?"

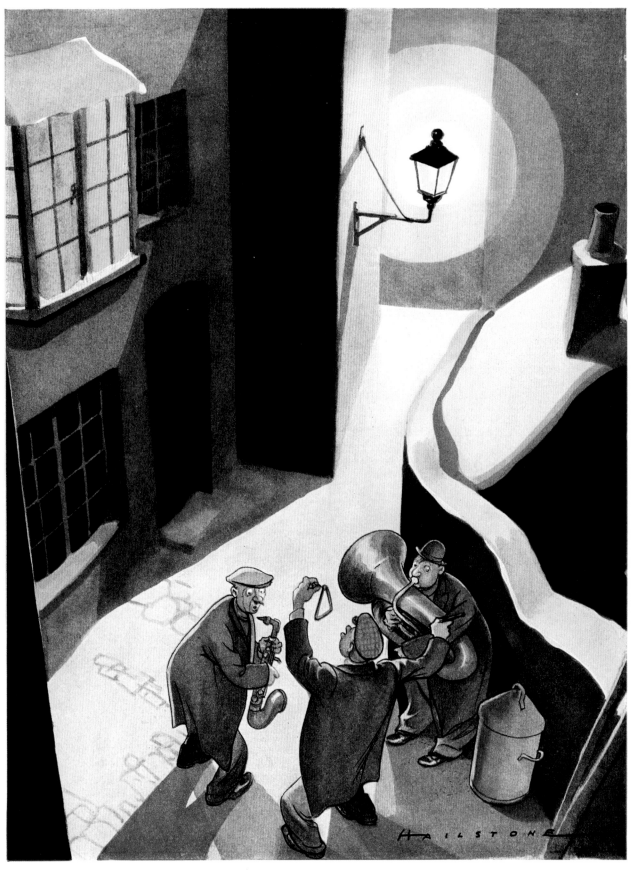

"'ERE A BIT MORE PIANOISSIMO ON THAT BLOOMIN' TRIANGLE, BERT; WE DON'T WANT
TO FRIGHTEN 'EM!"

Harold William Hailstone, 1937

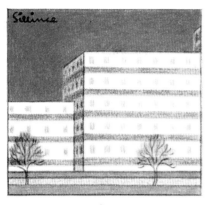

OF COURSE THE MODERN SERVICE FLATS MAY OFFER THE UNDOUBTED ADVANTAGES OF—

ELECTRIC LIFTS TO ALL FLOORS—        SQUASH COURTS—        SHOPS ON THE PREMISES—

RESTAURANTS—        CENTRAL HEATING AND—        CONSTANT HOT WATER—

BUT WHEN COMPARED WITH OLDER
HOMES—        HAVEN'T THEY JUST ONE—        SERIOUS SNAG?

William Augustus Sillince, 1938

CHRISTMAS DINNER IN THE BAY OF BISCAY

Douglas Lionel Mays, 1938

*"I had such a lovely dream last night—all in technicolor."*

Mervyn Wilson, 1941

**THE FIRST SAXOPHONIST**

Ernest Howard Shepard, 1938

**THE EARLIEST SURF-BATHER**

# IDEAL HOLIDAY

IT IS THE HEALTHY EXERCISE—

TOGETHER WITH THE WONDERFUL ALPINE SUN—

AND THE THRILL OF ACQUIRING SKILL AT A NEW SPORT—

ADDED TO THE EASE WITH WHICH ONE GETS TO KNOW PERFECT STRANGERS—

NOT FORGETTING THE SPICE OF DANGER IN A WINTER-SPORTS HOLIDAY—

THAT MAKE WINTER SUNSHINE CRUISES SO POPULAR.

Leslie Ilingworth, 1938

William Augustus Sillince, 1938

"WE REALLY *MUST* BE GOING NOW, DARLING; WE HAVE TO GET RIGHT OUT TO SURBITON."

"IT WAS JUST ABOUT HERE THAT EDWIN LOST A GOLD PENCIL LAST YEAR."

Harry Hewitt, 1938

Fougasse (Kenneth Bird), 1939

**RUSH HOUR**

**SUNLIGHT AND SHADOW**
Town

Pont (Graham Laidler), 1938

**SUNLIGHT AND SHADOW**

Country

THE FAMILY GOES AWAY

108

THE FAMILY COMES HOME

Ernest Howard Shepard, 1938

THE PRESERVED AMENITY

Thomas Derrick, 1937

E Seviour, 1939

"*Come in, Mr. Harris—the Lower Hickton Debating Society is in high fettle to-night.*"

Thomas Derrick, 1938

**INTERLUDE**

Frank Reynolds, 1938

"HOW FAR THAT LITTLE HEADLIGHT THROWS HIS BEAMS!"

113

Leslie Illingworth, 1938

"OH! . . . SORRY, I THOUGHT THESE SEATS WERE FREE."

# Art for Art's Sake I

*P*unch's artists didn't have to look far for inspiration and the world of art was always a fertile pool to dip into, even in the days of black and white. With the arrival of colour, call it parody or homage – patrons, painters and high art were even better game. Here 'Old Master' Frank Reynolds takes on another, spoofing Vermeer's *Lady Standing at a Virginal*, while Pont pities the artist who hasn't quite interpreted his patron's brief.

114

A LADY AT THE IVORIES *(after Vermeer)*.

Frank Reynolds, 1926

"I SAID I'M SORRY, PROFESSOR, BUT IT ISN'T AT ALL WHAT I MEANT."

Pont (Graham Laidler), 1937

**GUEST ROOM IN THE EAST WING**

1. MIDNIGHT

Anton (Antonia Yeoman), 1939

## GUEST ROOM IN THE EAST WING
### 2. Morning

Douglas Lionel Mays, 1939

*"We'll be down in a minute—Mummy's doing her ANTICS."*

Thomas Derrick, 1939

"*The afternoon Post* ALWAYS *does that.*"

Rowland Emett, 1942

Anton (Antonia Yeoman), 1942

*"This bit somehow always reminds me of Elfin Copse, just behind Little Chipping church."*

PRIMAVERA . . .

. . . PASSES BY.

Ernest Howard Shepard, 1939

124

Pont (Graham Laidler), 1939

THE SUMMER EXCURSION

JAS (William James Affleck Shepherd), 1939

THE BONE

Fougasse (Kenneth Bird), 1940

Anton (Antonia Yeoman), 1939

128

THE TENNIS PARTY AND—

129

Pont (Graham Laidler), 1940

**—THE GUST OF WIND**

*The Traffic problem in the United States is entirely and absolutely different to ours—*

*—it comes from an entirely and absolutely different direction.*

Fougasse (Kenneth Bird), 1939

BUREAU DE CHANGE

131

Harry Hewitt, 1940

HOSPITALITY—

—RETURNED

Anton (Antonia Yeoman), 1940

134

"I dunno 'ow it come 'ere. I found it in my field on Boxin' Day."

George Morrow, 1941

Fougasse (Kenneth Bird), 1944

"NOW WHO SHALL WE CHOOSE FOR SANTA CLAUS?"

Harold William Hailstone, 1936

Pont (Graham Laidler), 1941

**NEW YEAR'S MORNING**

# Anton (Antonia Yeoman (1907–1970)

'Anton' began as a sister/brother collaboration in 1937 (with Harold Underwood Thompson [1911–1996]) – but as they once wrote: 'please don't ask us how it happens'. During the Second World War Harold contributed only gags, and in 1949 Anton became entirely Antonia.

*"So I put it to you, m'lud, that a breach of promise has been proved."*

*" I could use the juggler."*

Anton (Antonia Yeoman), 1943

# The Second World War

As they joined the armed forces or engaged in war work that left little time for drawing, the conflict scattered *Punch*'s artists around the globe. Yet, with the older generation making their contribution, the magazine still managed to publish some of its most stunning colour images during those wartime years.

HOME THOUGHTS FROM ABROAD

John Whitfield Taylor, 1940

Fougasse (Kenneth Bird), 1940

*" Well, for Heaven's sake, don't* look *in their direction."*
*" But how can I* drive *if I don't ? "*

I

142

II

# WELCOME FOR THE WARRIOR RETURNING FROM THE WARS
## AN HISTORICAL SURVEY

III

IV

Pont (Graham Laidler), 1940

PUNCH SUMMER NUMBER

E.H. Shepard

Ernest Howard Shepard, 1940

145

Douglas (Douglas England), 1940

FREEDOM

Leslie Illingworth, 1940

**COMBAT**

148

Douglas Lionel Mays, 1946

*"So you see, dear, one* can *be* decorative *and* useful.*"*

**THE FARMER'S IDEA OF THE LANDGIRL**

**THE LANDGIRL'S IDEA OF THE FARMER**

Leslie Illingworth, 1940

150

Harold William Hailstone, 1940

*"I knew I'd hung the darn thing somewhere."*

Douglas Lionel Mays, 1941

*" So I joined the A.F.S."*

William Augustus Sillince, 1941

Russell Brockbank, 1941

Leslie Illingworth, 1942

*When one's a Subaltern, the world is full of Captains:*

*When one becomes a Captain, one's entirely surrounded by Majors:*

*When one gets one's majority, one finds one's living in a world of Colonels:*

*And if, at long last, one reaches the exalted rank of Colonel . . . Generals ! ! !*

Fougasse (Kenneth Bird), 1941

NOISE 1841

NOISE 1941

Ernest Howard Shepard, 1941

Harry Hewitt, 1943

Fougasse (Kenneth Bird), 1942

*" Yes—my husband is engaged on work of national importance."*

160

Mervyn Wilson, 1944

"That's Gilchrist—in charge of post-war planning."

Lawrence 'Lawrie' Siggs, 1943

*"And this time next year what will they say?   It'll be 'Improve on whatever you done last year.'"*

DOUGLAS.

162

Douglas (Douglas England), 1943

**ONE HUNDRED PER CENT.**

Frank Reynolds, 1943

Acanthus (Harold Frank Hoar), 1945

*"Say, it's grand to meet another steel-frame erector."*

William Augustus Sillince, 1941

Rowland Emett, 1942

168

Leslie Illingworth, 1944

*"Purely from a publicity point of view, the necessity for camouflage suits us very well."*

*"No, Albert, you mustn't talk to Mum now!"*

Frank Reynolds, 1944

John Whitfield Taylor, 1944

"*The ironic* part is that it's no change for me — I used to come here every year."

| January | | February | | March | | April | | May | | June | |
|---|---|---|---|---|---|---|---|---|---|---|---|
| S | . 2 . 9 . 16 . 23 . 30 | S | . . . 6 . 13 . 20 . 27 | S | . . . 5 . 12 . 19 . 26 | S | . 2 . 9 . 16 . 23 . 30 | S | . . . 7 . 14 . 21 . 28 | S | . . . . 4 . 11 . 18 . 25 |
| M | . 3 . 10 . 17 . 24 . 31 | M | . . . 7 . 14 . 21 . 28 | M | . . . 6 . 13 . 20 . 27 | M | . 3 . 10 . 17 . 24 . . . | M | . 1 . 8 . 15 . 22 . 29 | M | . . . 5 . 12 . 19 . 26 |
| Tu | . 4 . 11 . 18 . 25 . . . | Tu | . 1 . 8 . 15 . 22 . 29 | Tu | . . . 7 . 14 . 21 . 28 | Tu | . 4 . 11 . 18 . 25 . . . | Tu | . 2 . 9 . 16 . 23 . 30 | Tu | . . . 6 . 13 . 20 . 27 |
| W | . 5 . 12 . 19 . 26 . . . | W | . 2 . 9 . 16 . 23 . . . | W | . 1 . 8 . 15 . 22 . 29 | W | . 5 . 12 . 19 . 26 . . . | W | . 3 . 10 . 17 . 24 . 31 | W | . . . 7 . 14 . 21 . 28 |
| Th | . 6 . 13 . 20 . 27 . . . | Th | . 3 . 10 . 17 . 24 . . . | Th | . 2 . 9 . 16 . 23 . 30 | Th | . 6 . 13 . 20 . 27 . . . | Th | . 4 . 11 . 18 . 25 . . . | Th | . 1 . 8 . 15 . 22 . 29 |
| F | . 7 . 14 . 21 . 28 . . . | F | . 4 . 11 . 18 . 25 . . . | F | . 3 . 10 . 17 . 24 . 31 | F | . 7 . 14 . 21 . 28 . . . | F | . 5 . 12 . 19 . 26 . . . | F | . 2 . 9 . 16 . 23 . 30 |
| S | 1 . 8 . 15 . 22 . 29 . . . | S | . 5 . 12 . 19 . 26 . . . | S | . 4 . 11 . 18 . 25 . . . | S | 1 . 8 . 15 . 22 . 29 . . . | S | . 6 . 13 . 20 . 27 . . . | S | . 3 . 10 . 17 . 24 . . . |

| July | | August | | September | | October | | November | | December | |
|---|---|---|---|---|---|---|---|---|---|---|---|
| S | . 2 . 9 . 16 . 23 . 30 | S | . . . 6 . 13 . 20 . 27 | S | . . . 3 . 10 . 17 . 24 | S | . 1 . 8 . 15 . 22 . 29 | S | . . . 5 . 12 . 19 . 26 | S | . 3 . 10 . 17 . 24 . 31 |
| M | . 3 . 10 . 17 . 24 . 31 | M | . . . 7 . 14 . 21 . 28 | M | . . . 4 . 11 . 18 . 25 | M | . 2 . 9 . 16 . 23 . 30 | M | . . . 6 . 13 . 20 . 27 | M | . 4 . 11 . 18 . 25 . . . |
| Tu | . 4 . 11 . 18 . 25 . . . | Tu | . 1 . 8 . 15 . 22 . 29 | Tu | . . . 5 . 12 . 19 . 26 | Tu | . 3 . 10 . 17 . 24 . 31 | Tu | . . . 7 . 14 . 21 . 28 | Tu | . 5 . 12 . 19 . 26 . . . |
| W | . 5 . 12 . 19 . 26 . . . | W | . 2 . 9 . 16 . 23 . 30 | W | . . . 6 . 13 . 20 . 27 | W | . 4 . 11 . 18 . 25 . . . | W | . 1 . 8 . 15 . 22 . 29 | W | . 6 . 13 . 20 . 27 . . . |
| Th | . 6 . 13 . 20 . 27 . . . | Th | . 3 . 10 . 17 . 24 . 31 | Th | . . . 7 . 14 . 21 . 28 | Th | . 5 . 12 . 19 . 26 . . . | Th | . 2 . 9 . 16 . 23 . 30 | Th | . 7 . 14 . 21 . 28 . . . |
| F | . 7 . 14 . 21 . 28 . . . | F | . . . 1 . 8 . 15 . 22 . 29 | F | . 1 . 8 . 15 . 22 . 29 | F | . 6 . 13 . 20 . 27 . . . | F | . 3 . 10 . 17 . 24 . . . | F | 1 . 8 . 15 . 22 . 29 . . . |
| S | 1 . 8 . 15 . 22 . 29 . . . | S | . 5 . 12 . 19 . 26 . . . | S | . 2 . 9 . 16 . 23 . 30 | S | . 7 . 14 . 21 . 28 . . . | S | . 4 . 11 . 18 . 25 . . . | S | 2 . 9 . 16 . 23 . 30 . . . |

Douglas Lionel Mays, 1942

Fougasse (Kenneth Bird), 1945

173

**THE UNCHANGING FACE OF BRITAIN**

# 1946–1955
## THE POST-WAR WORLD

Rowland Emett, 1947

*". . . and if they draws us into this Railway Nationalization scheme, BANG goes our individuality!"*

175

Frank Reynolds, 1945

*" Mushrooms—springing up like prefabs ! "*

Rowland Emett, 1949

*"Yes, I've heard of* LOTS *of happily retired chaps being suddenly dragged back into harness . . ."*

178

*"I don't think you've quite hit off Edwin."*

Mervyn Wilson, 1949

Norman Mansbridge, 1947

*"Some uncanny instinct brings them back here summer after summer."*

"I advise you to snap it up before the National Trust gets wind of it."

John Whitfield Taylor, 1948

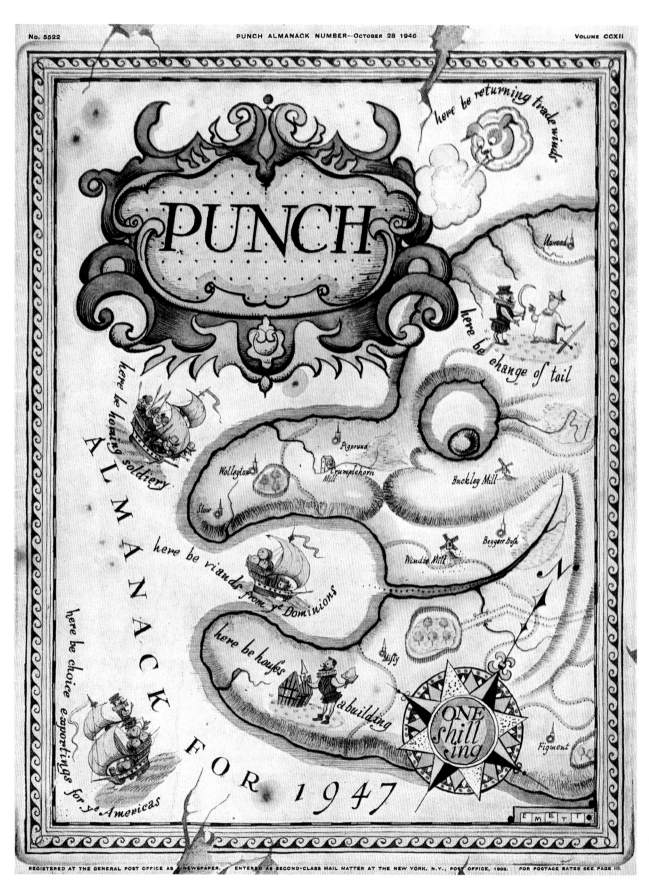

181

Rowland Emett, 1947

"I'm meeting her on the pier after the show"

Mervyn Wilson, 1947

Anton (Antonia Yeoman), 1945

*"A Mrs. Abercrombie in the second row wants to know where you got that dress."*

184

Russell Brockbank, 1950

*"No, sir, it ain't gale-force till the tree touches the 'ouse."*

William Augustus Sillince, 1950

# Rowland Emett (1906–1990)

Emett's delicately whimsical style featuring his favourite eccentric machines evolved on the pages of 1940s *Punch*, to which he was on an exclusive contract.

By 1951 Emett had become a household name with the construction of his *Far Tottering and Oystercreek Railway* at that year's Festival of Britain.

Rowland Emett, 1946

*"Every time us 'as a bumper catch* THIS *'appens."*

Rowland Emett, 1949

187

188

*"Aye, the Afternoon Slow is* ALWAYS *an 'elp with Top Meadow."*

Rowland Emett, 1945

Douglas Lionel Mays, 1950

*"You'll have to excuse the mess - we've got the painters in."*

MISTAKEN VIEWS OF THE BRITISH

IV. THE BRITISH

Fougasse (Kenneth Bird), 1951

Norman Mansbridge, 1950

"... *And if you hear a long, pitiful cry, with* NO *rattling chains — it's Baby.*"

Russell Brockbank, 1953

Ionicus (Joshua Armitage), 1948

194

*" That's rather too much.   Have you got the runner-up?"*

William Augustus Sillince, 1950

Rowland Emett, 1950

Douglas Lionel Mays, 1953

"Your wife still on holiday, old man?"

Norman Mansbridge, 1951

Russell Brockbank, 1952

Ernest Howard Shepard, 1951

Rowland Emett, 1952

*"I should snap it up, gentlemen! There are two other Services interested . . ."*

202

Gerard Hoffnung, 1954

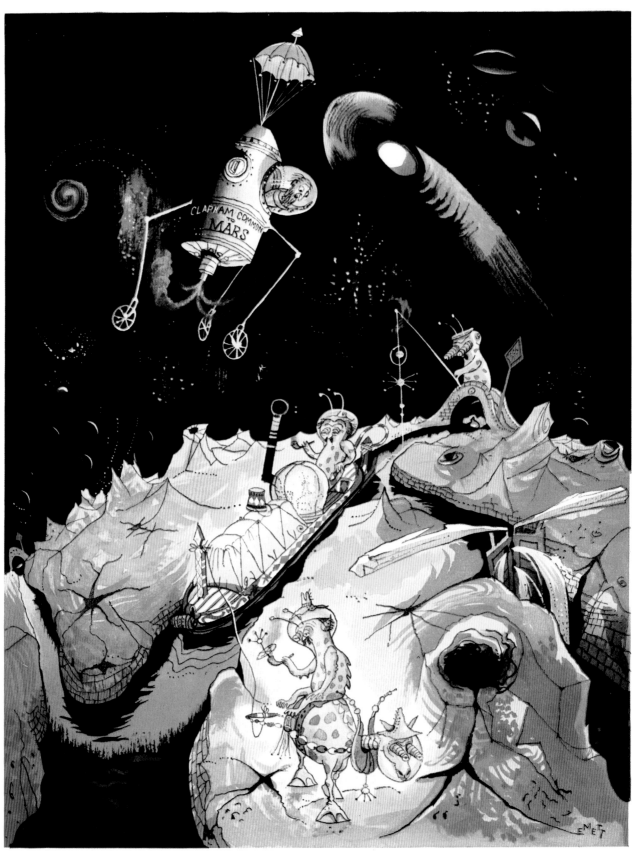

*"Not **barges**, Charlie - narrow boats."*

Rowland Emett, 1948

"*I TOLD you never to take the 11.50 round by the Witch Hollow loop . . . !*"

# The Royal Family II
## The Coronation 1953

The young Queen Elizabeth's coronation in 1953 moved *Punch* to produce a souvenir Coronation Number with colour contributions from some of its finest artists, starting with a flowery Fougasse cover. The pastel palette continued with illustrations like Douglas Mays' delightful tribute to the Royal children, Charles and Anne, setting off on their storybook path to the future. E H Shepard's exquisite depiction of the English countryside (overleaf) was one of his final contributions to the magazine.

**ROYAL ROAD TO THE FUTURE**

Douglas Lionel Mays, 1953

Fougasse (Kenneth Bird), 1953

## MADRIGAL FOR JUNE

Come, Nature, sing your madrigal
    with double music of delight.
O greensleeve trees be twice so green.
    dear maids of honour to the Queen:
sing twice so sweetly, blackbirds, call
    upon the English flowers that pight
these very meadows in her namesake's day
    to be in this sweet season twice so gay.

Brooks that with lazy-daisy stitch
    the patchwork fields together sew
do you sing too with voices clear
    delighting day—and us—to hear:
the sun will give your singing-pitch—
now sharp, now flat, now high, now low—
    when his gold tuning-fork vibrates
    and all his music co-relates.

But, Nature, if you do not choose—
    to be all gold and green and gay
and will not sing as sing you should
through bird and brook, in field and wood—
    do not ungraciously refuse—
        but send a dove-soft day,
and we will sing, her people all.
    her name—itself a madrigal.
                                    R.C.S.

209

Ernest Howard Shepard, 1953

William Hewison, 1953

André François, 1953

*"What do you mean, 'not ideal circumstances'?"*

Rowland Emett, 1951

*"And now perhaps a quick word from Driver Firebrace, who is determined that the Yuletide mail shall get through on time…"*

Mervyn Wilson, 1954

Holiday Prospects

Russell Brockbank, 1955

215

Fougasse (Kenneth Bird), 1953

*Promenade des Anglais*

*"Then of course as the tide goes out, they get trapped."*

Norman Thelwell, 1953

Norman Thelwell, 1954

No. 5948     PUNCH, SEPTEMBER 15 1954     Vol. CCXXVII

# PUNCH

## Autumn Number

DIZ

Edward Ardizzone, 1954

Rowland Emett, 1954

" . . . and here is the news . . . During last night's severe gale Shrimphaven pier was entirely washed away . . ."

220

William Scully, 1954

"Waiter, we still don't seem to have an ash-tray."

*"Such a pity the visiting bellringers can't be at the party . . ."*

Rowland Emett, 1954

222

Edward Ardizzone, 1954

*"Genuine English tourists, monsieur, working our passage to the Côte d'Or."*

Rowland Emett, 1953

224

George Sprod, 1956

226

Russell Brockbank, 1957

THE INTERNATIONAL GEOPHYSICAL YEAR, 1957

228

Ronald Searle, 1956

229

Jan Lewitt, 1956

230

Smilby (Francis Wilford-Smith), 1956

# André François (1915–2005)

André François (born Farkas) came to Paris as an art student before the Second World War, via Timis,oara and Budapest. One of the world's greatest graphic artists, François began contributing to *Punch* in the 1950s and produced some of the magazine's most memorable covers.

André François, 1955

*" Overdoing things as usual."*

*One of the nicest things about English sport—*

*is the way the artist has always been able—*

*to introduce a note of grace and harmony—*

*into his work.*

Michael ffolkes (Brian Davis), 1956

Rowland Emett, 1956

Steadman, Ralph, 1961

William Scully, 1960

Searle, Ronald, 1960

Quentin Blake, 1959

238

André François, 1957

Smilby (Francis Wilford-Smith), 1956

smilby.

*As a result of myxomatosis, foxes are becoming as savage as wolves…*

240

*and birds, owing to the Protection of Birds Act, are losing their fear of man; so that…*

*before long, life in the countryside...*

Norman Thelwell, 1956

No. 6153      PUNCH, JULY 23 1958      VOL. CCXXXV

# Punch

**9d**

Ronald Searle, 1958

William Augustus Sillince, 1960

# Ronald Searle (1920–2011)
## Heroes of Our Time:

Among *Punch*'s most celebrated caricatures were Ronald Searle's *Heroes of Our Time* of 1956–1957, just one of the brilliant series the artist produced for the magazine. Like *People in Punch* in the 1930s, these were collectables, published as centre-fold double page spreads. Once again the 12 sitters came from the current crop of the great, the good and the famous.

Ronald Searle, 1957

*9. Sir Laurence Olivier and Vivien Leigh*

*5. T S Eliot*

*7. HRH Princess Margaret*

*1. Sir Malcolm Sargent*

*12. Lord Russell*

*4. Aneurin Bevan*

Ronald Searle, 1956–57

No. 6161      PUNCH, OCTOBER 29 1958      Vol. CCXXXV

# Punch

9<u>d</u>

*Adamson*

George Adamson, 1958

Jean Michel Folon, 1957

248

No. 6087　　　　　　　　PUNCH, APRIL 24 1957　　　　　　　　Vol. CCXXXII

# Punch

**9ᵈ**

Quentin Blake, 1957

# Norman Thelwell (1923–2004)

The man who created the 'Thelwell pony' was far more than an artist of small girls and their podgy steeds. Thelwell contributed over 1,500 cartoons to *Punch* and his colour work for the magazine included dozens of covers and some wonderful depictions of the British countryside.

*"I'll take this one."*

Norman Thelwell, 1960

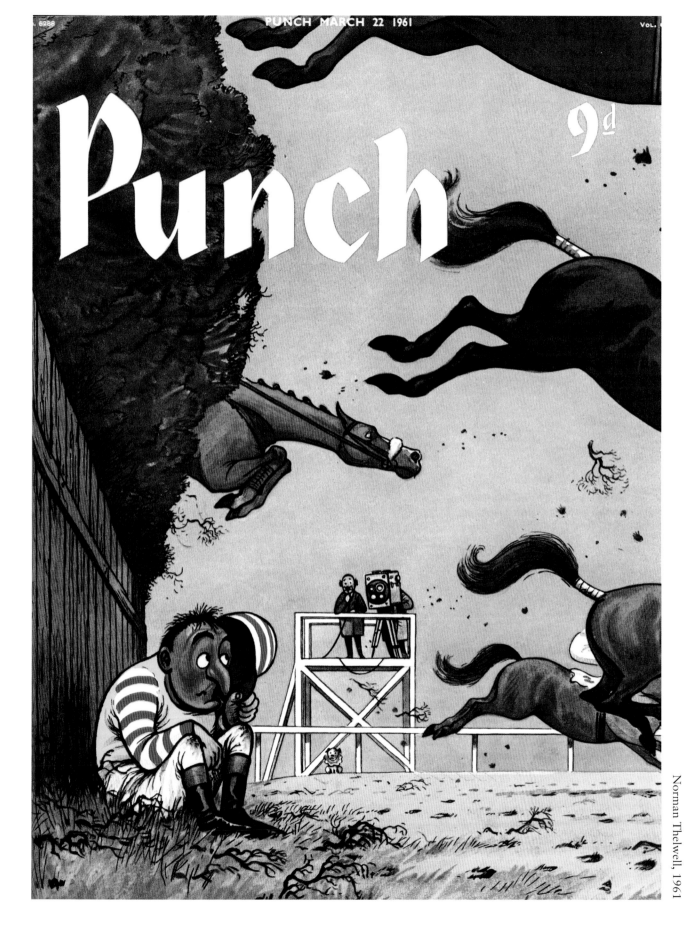

Norman Thelwell, 1961

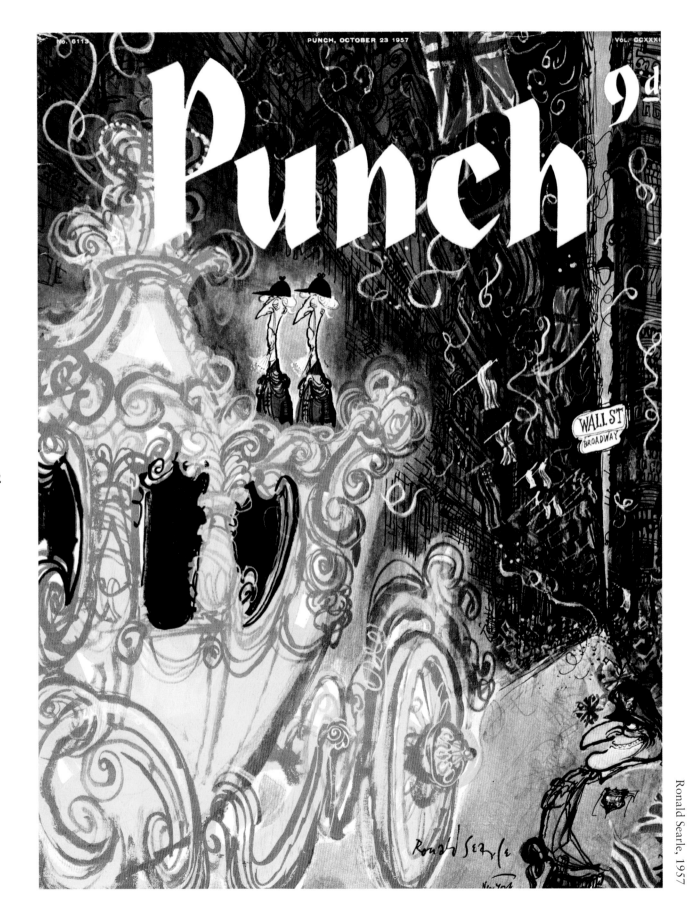

Ronald Searle, 1957

Jean-Jacques Sempé, 1958

254

No. 6221                    PUNCH, DECEMBER 16 1959                    Vol. CCXXXVII

William Hewison, 1959

256

Russell Brockbank, 1962

257

Bruce Petty, 1958

**1958**

**1959**

Norman Thelwell, 1959

No. 6185          PUNCH, FEBRUARY 25 1959          Vol. CCXXXVI

259

Kenneth Mahood, 1959

# PUNCH ALMANACK 1960

260

Michael ffolkes (Brian Davis), 1960

*"We beat them, they beat us — I forget the details."*

No. 6174      PUNCH, DECEMBER 10 1958      VOL. CCXXXV

261

Maurice Bartlett, 1958

Ronald Searle, 1958

*"I have the temperament, but not the physique."*

William Hewison, 1959

André François, 1962

NO. 6260     PUNCH SEPTEMBER 14 1960     VOL. CCXXXIX

# Punch

**9d**

265

Jean-Jacques Sempé, 1960

George Adamson, 1961

William Scully, 1960

*"The forecast did say 'and bright intervals'."*

Punch

29 MAY 1963     ONE SHILLING

SUMMER NUMBER

TRY YOUR LUCK

GRAND FAIR

Leslie Wood, 1963

269

Jean-Jacques Sempé, 1960

270

George Adamson, 1963

271

Kenneth Mahood, 1963

Kenneth Mahood, 1962

Jean-Jacques Sempé, 1961

Russell Brockbank, 1961

Ronald Searle, 1961

277

Quentin Blake, 1958

278

# Spring, the sweet Spring . . .

*. . . is the year's pleasant king;*
*Then blooms each thing, then maids dance in a ring,*
*Cold doth not sting, the pretty birds do sing —*
*Cuckoo, jug-jug, pu-we, to-witta-woo!*

PUNCH, April 18 1962

The palm and may make country houses gay,
Lambs frisk and play, the shepherds pipe all day,
And we hear aye birds tune this merry lay—
Cuckoo, jug-jug, pu-we, to-witta-woo!

279

The fields breathe sweet, the daisies kiss our feet,
Young lovers meet, old wives a-sunning sit,
In every street these tunes our ears do greet—
Cuckoo, jug-jug, pu-we, to-witta-woo!
Spring! the sweet Spring!

Gerald Scarfe, 1962

280

André François, 1957

André François, 1963

Russell Brockbank, 1960

Anton (Antonia Yeoman), 1960

'*Usually when Harold tries to repair something, he only makes it worse.*'

Punch

31 JULY 1963          ONE SHILLING

ff after Manet

Michael ffolkes (Brian Davis), 1963

"*My lease stipulates no pets.*"

Quentin Blake, 1963

Norman Thelwell, 1967

287

William Hewison, 1960

*"Have you something a little less frivolous?"*

## I—STATUS BY BIRTH

*This obsolescent form of inherited status is marked by a tendency towards the tall, narrow, and angular, and a general air of not having bothered to impress.*

Ronald Searle, 1960

## II—STATUS BY POSSESSION

*The emphasis here is on the low, long and sleek. Somebody has obviously bothered a good deal.*

Punch

**19 SEPTEMBER 1962    ONE SHILLING**

**AUTUMN NUMBER**

Smilby (Francis Wilford-Smith), 1962

Maurice Bartlett, 1962

292

Quentin Blake, 1962

*The sad decline in cricket attendances* is hardly surprising
After all the game is only made up of some of this

and one of these ● six of these ▮ four of these ⬮ two of these ⬮ and two of these

and these

whilst the only stimulant permitted during the game is this →

Nowadays the clothes are hardly inspiring, the greatest visual extravagance being one of these ⬮ In the past when people actually went to cricket matches it was all more exciting. The players looked like this or this

(Even the shape of the bat was more amusing)

Everyone knows they do these things better abroad .....

..... where the turnstiles are never still. By comparison with this excitement and colour it is hardly surprising that people just stay away from our Summer game.

Except, of course, when the West Indians are here.

Michael ffolkes (Brian Davis), 1964

294

Norman Thelwell, 1963

295

Norman Thelwell, 1963

*"I'm afraid it's Spring again, Harold."*

Kenneth Mahood, 1962

# Punch

**5 SEPTEMBER 1962**    **ONE SHILLING**

PAW

PAV (Francis Minet), 1962

298

Barry, 1963

300

Michael ffolkes (Brian Davis), 1966

"*OK, Hendrix, you're through with your Blue Period!*"

William Scully, 1965

Smilby (Francis Wilford-Smith), 1964

304

Kenneth Mahood, 1964

4 AUGUST 1965
ONE SHILLING & SIXPENCE

MALCOLM BRADBURY'S Journey into Danger

# Punch

Quentin Blake, 1965

Ed McLachlan, 1963

Jean-Jacques Sempé, 1962

19 MAY 1965
ONE SHILLING & SIXPENCE

MALCOLM BRADBURY—Book Cults

# Punch

308

· EVENSONG ·
"pitch well maintained....."
—Church Times
"really swings ......"
—Melody Maker.

Geoffrey Dickinson

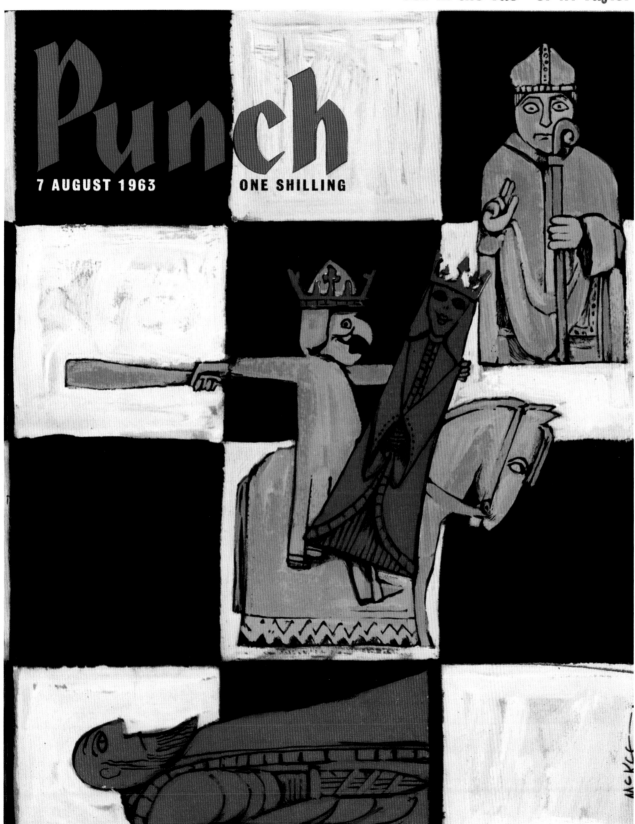

**Punch**

7 AUGUST 1963       ONE SHILLING

David McKee, 1963

# George Adamson (1913–2005)

One of Britain's most brilliant, prolific, yet little known illustrators, Adamson began contributing to *Punch* in 1939. Most striking of all his works for the magazine were the subtly inventive covers he produced in the 1950s and 1960s.

George Adamson, 1964

PUNCH 23 JULY 1969
TWO SHILLINGS

DOWN AMONG THE MET-MEN

# Punch

MTrevithick

Michael Trevithick, 1969

313

Geoffrey Dickinson, 1963

PUNCH 23 NOVEMBER 1966
ONE SHILLING & SIXPENCE

**A BEATLE talks to Patrick Catling**

314

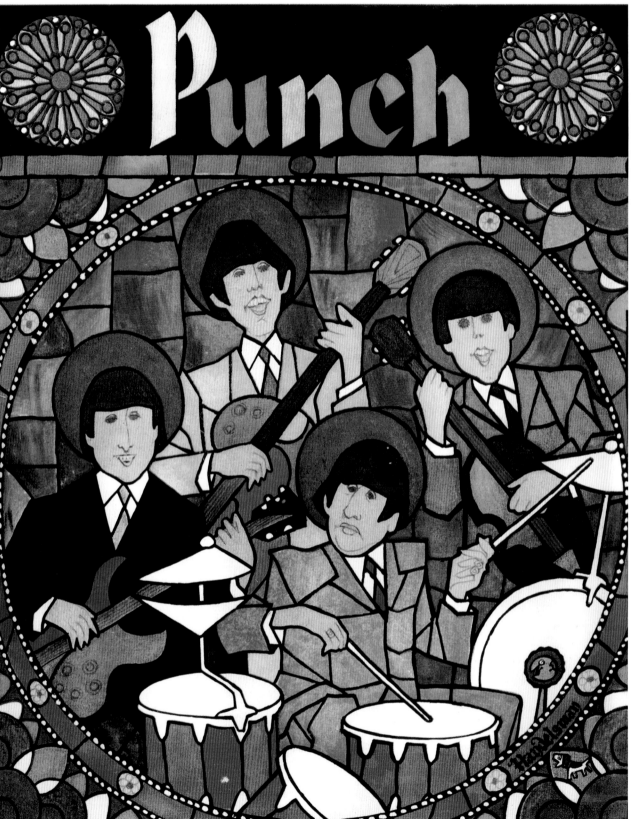

John Bernard Handelsman, 1965

PUNCH 30 JULY 1969
TWO SHILLINGS

SELLING BRITAIN ABROAD

# Punch

BRITISH WEEK

Geoffrey Dickinson, 1969

# 1970–1992
## THE SEVENTIES AND BEYOND

Michael Heath, 1971

**PUNCH 19—25 MAY 1971**
**12½p WEEKLY**

**This week : SO YOU WANT TO ESCAPE?**

Ross (Harry Ross Thomson), 1971

21—27 JUNE 1972    15p WEEKLY

# Punch

## Report from America:
# WHO WILL THEY VOTE FOR?

Geoffrey Dickinson, 1972

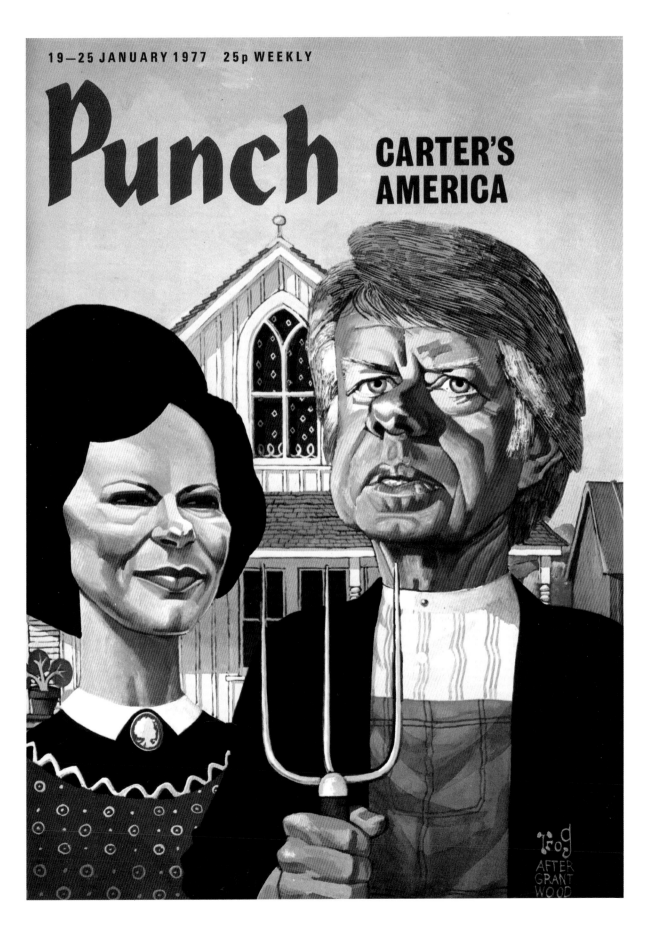

19—25 JANUARY 1977    25p WEEKLY

# Punch    CARTER'S AMERICA

Trog (Walter 'Wally' Fawkes), 1977

# Trog (Wally Fawkes) (b. 1924)

The cartoonist who is also a brilliant jazz musician (and vice versa), Trog's stunning caricatures of the celebrities and politicians of the day were a mainstay of *Punch* covers of the 1970s.

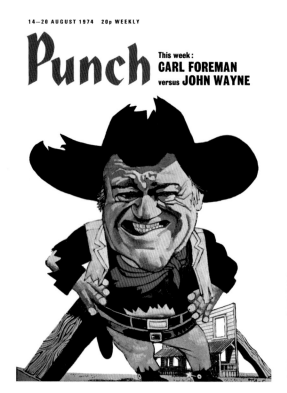

Trog (Walter 'Wally' Fawkes), 1976

Stan McMurtry, 1974

9 – 15 MAY 1973    15p WEEKLY

# Punch

**This week:**
# THE TYRANNY OF THE TELEPHONE

323

John Jensen, 1973

# The Royal Family III
## The Silver Jubilee 1977

By the 1970s *Punch* was not quite so reverent of the monarchy as it used to be, and Ed McLachlan knocks the commercialism of the Queen's Silver Jubilee with his wind-up royals. Its 'souvenir' number is far from respectful with Pearly Queen Elizabeth and her Pearly Consort, Prince Philip, having a jolly knees-up.

Ed McLachlan, 1977

25p

# Punch

## JUBILEE NUMBER

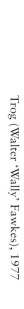

Trog (Walter 'Wally' Fawkes), 1977

September 12, 1984 · WEEKLY · 65p

BIG BUSINESS NUMBER

Arnold Roth, 1984

John Jensen, 1989

328

Ed McLachlan, 1990

Mike Williams, 1987

*"Oh God! What's Walter brought back this time?"*

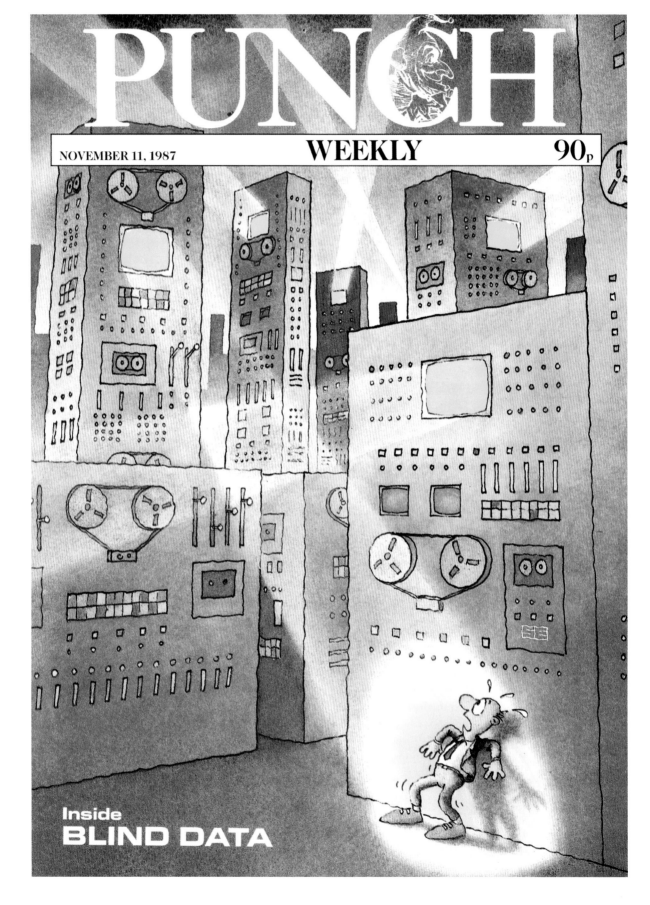

'Listen, kid - money is at the root of all evil, not apples!'

Alan de la Nougerede, 1990

Roy Raymonde, 1986

Bud Grace, 1984

Eli (Eli Bauer), 1986

*"Hey, guys! It's Yuppy!"*

*'Well that's the last of the Mohicans. There's still a bit of Sioux left, if anyone's interested'*

Mike Williams, 1990

334

Stan Eales, 1990

'Uh oh...'

Tony Reeve, 1992

336

'They think the killer is still on the premises, sarge'

Ed McLachlan, 1991

Holte (Trevor Holder), 1985

Ian Jackson, 1984

TORVILL AND MUJAHEDIN

Steve Way,, 1989

'Well, somebody ordered cable.'

Mike Williams, 1990

Mike Williams, 1991

'True, true, but on the downside, I spend a fortune on condoms'

# Mike Williams (b. 1940)

**W**illiams began cartooning for *Punch* in 1967, becoming its cartoon editor 30 years later. One of the world's great cartoonists, his inspiration comes from practically anywhere, though historical themes were always a particular favourite.

*Meet the Neighbours! An East German's guide to West Europeans*

*"Oh, him? Well, it was pretty exciting really. He nibbled through the rotten skirting-board and got squashed under a pile of my pornographic magazines."*

343

Mike Williams, 1989

'Delbert very nearly made it as a pop star in the Sixties.'

**FUNNY, INTELLIGENT, SAME TIME SAME CHANNEL**

28TH JULY 1989   £1 · US $2.95

# PUNCH

**JOKERS WILD!**

344

ZAP!!
ROBIN,
BOY-WONDER:
DOWN AND OUT
AND INTERVIEWED

POW!!
BUG BONANZA:
WILL YOU
WAKE UP
AS A
COCKROACH?

**AT PUNCH**

ISSN 0033-4278

30

9 770033 427006

Graham Higgins, 1989

Robert Wilson, 1988

*"Just watch where you're putting your feet."*

Holte (Trevor Holder), 1988

'Forget the Crepe Suzette, Minchin - I'll have the rice-pudding.'

"Mr McGregor's got a Flymo!"

Neil Bennett, 1989

'You've been at the Laura Ashley catalogue again!'

Ed McLachlan, 1991

# The Royal Family IV
## The Diana Factor

*P*unch (and practically everyone else) found a new princess to adore with the arrival of Diana among the Royals. The magazine's disenchantment with the monarchy didn't extend to the Princess of Wales and she became a regular fixture on *Punch* covers on her journey from Shy Di to triumphant conqueror of Britain and the New World to wronged woman.

Trog (Walter 'Wally' Fawkes), 1981

348

David Smith, 1985

Unknown, 1990

349

David Hughes, 1991

'Vlad the Impaler may be a tyrant but you can't beat his lavish cocktail parties'

Martin Ross, 1991

*Passing Through – David Attenborough*

Trog (Walter 'Wally' Fawkes), 1987

# Art for Art's Sake II

Fascinated as ever by the world of art, *Punch*'s artists were still going strong in the late 20th century. Stan Eales' Warhol-esque cave painter is ahead of his time, while Jonathan Pugh shows what really lay behind Picasso's Blue Period. Meanwhile, High Art turns its nose up at Modernism in Alan de la Nougerede's look at a new acquisition by an art gallery.

Jonathan Pugh, 1991

*Picasso's Blue Period*

352

Stan Eales, 1991

Alan de la Nougerede, 1990

'Well, there goes the neighbourhood!'

Ray Lowry, 1986

*"Relax, Simpkins. What's the point of having money if you can't enjoy it?"*

354

Ray Lowry, 1989

Roy Raymonde, 1987

355

Tony Reeve, 1988

356

William Haefeli, 1991

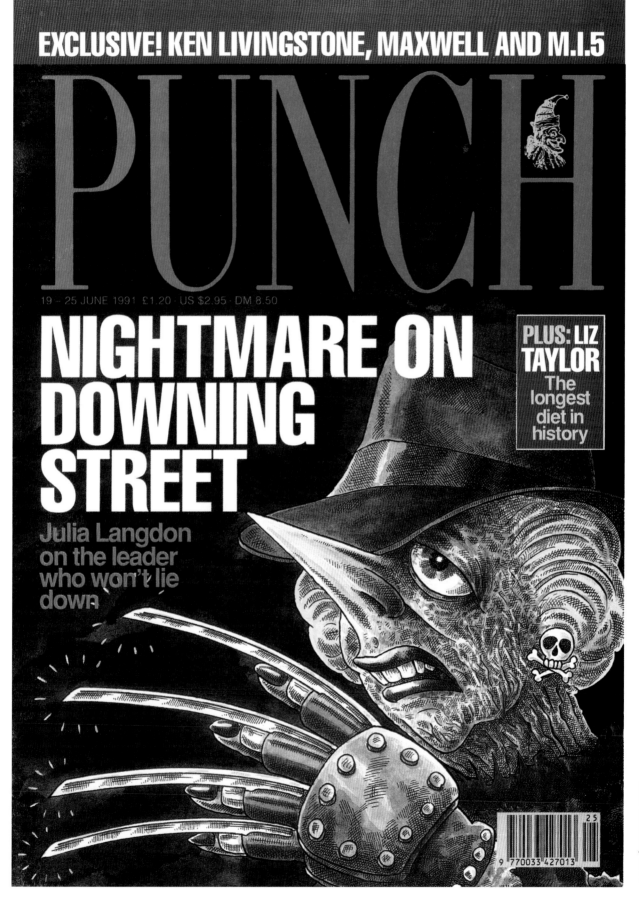

**EXCLUSIVE! KEN LIVINGSTONE, MAXWELL AND M.I.5**

# PUNCH

19 – 25 JUNE 1991 · £1.20 · US $2.95 · DM 8.50

## NIGHTMARE ON DOWNING STREET

Julia Langdon on the leader who won't lie down

**PLUS: LIZ TAYLOR** The longest diet in history

Paul Thomas, 1991

Tony Husband, 1988

*"God, what a dump!"*

Robert Wilson, 1990

'...but I thought somebody was doing something about that bloody hole.'

# SPECIAL COLLECTOR'S EDITION
# PUNCH

**150TH ANNIVERSARY · 17 JULY 1841 ~ 17 JULY 1991**

Ralph Steadman, 1991

**£1.20** **(US $2.95 · DM 8.50)**

*'Remember the Bay City Rollers?'*

Ed McLachlan, 1992

# Stan Eales (b. 1962)

New Zealander Stan Eales had his very first contribution to *Punch* in 1987 published on the coveted cover spot. Although Eales has drawn gags on many subjects, he is perhaps best known as the eco-cartoonist *par excellence*.

Stan Eales, 1988

Stan Eales, 1990

Stan Eales, 1990

*'One day son, all of this will be hamburgers'*

'I just love fast food.'

Mike Williams, 1990

Stan Eales, 1990

Robert Wilson, 1989

*'All right, have it your way, it's something to do with the greenhouse effect.'*

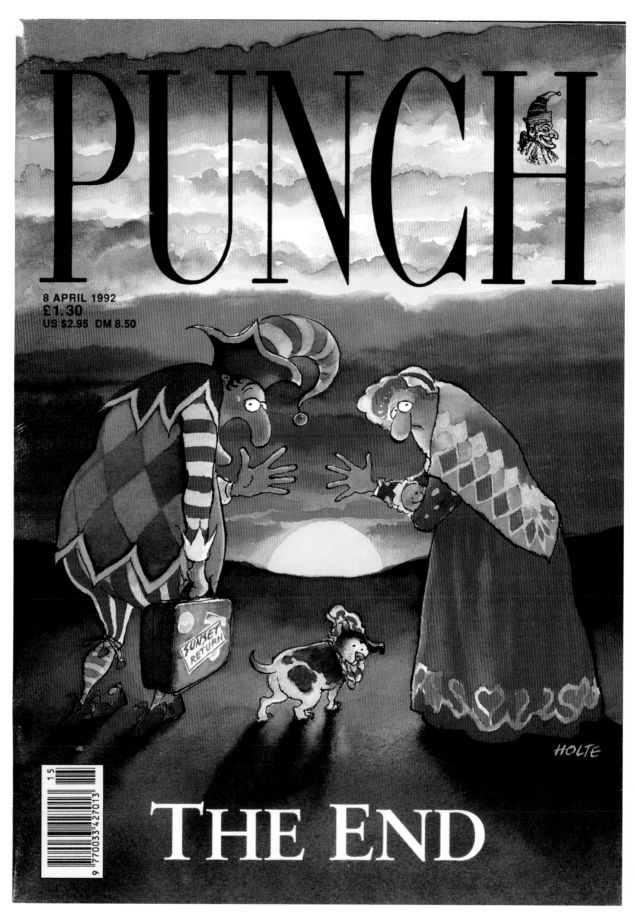

Holte (Trevor Holder), 1992

# INDEX

Mike Williams, 1991